Christmas 2014

Dear Beth,
   I hope you enjoy this as much as I have. So many wonderful memories and you are a part of all of them.

Love you,
Jennifer

Day 352 – Overrun
Saturday, August 11, 2012, 1:34 p.m.
Sunrise: 6:50 a.m.   Sunset: 8:52 p.m.

View366

A Year-long Visual Story of the St. Joseph Lighthouses

by Laura Kraklau

Copyright © 2014 by Laura Kraklau

Photography and narration: Laura Kraklau

Book design and layout: Michael Johnson

Copy editing and proofreading: Jennifer Cruickshank, Jannette Yergeau

Printing: Holland Litho Printing Service, Zeeland, Michigan

Published by View 366 LLC, P.O. Box 382, 1101 Broad Street, Suite 314,
St. Joseph, MI 49085

ISBN 978-0-692-21032-1

First Edition
Printed in the United States of America
September 2014

Many of the photos in this book are available as prints.
For more information visit **www.view366.com**.

Day 16 – Ride Off into the Sunset
Saturday, September 10, 2011, 8:03 p.m.
Sunrise: 7:20 a.m.   Sunset: 8:05 p.m.

Day 18 – Finished for the Day

Monday, September 12, 2011, 8:02 p.m.
Sunrise: 7:22 a.m.   Sunset: 8:01 p.m.

Introduction

They began life serving the maritime industry as beacons of safe passage. As technology progressed over the decades, their utilitarian role diminished. Yet, interest in and love for these beautiful and important structures has increased over time.

The dual range lighthouses in St. Joseph, Michigan, have become iconic symbols of the southwestern Michigan town that is home to 8,300 residents and the destination of tens of thousands of visitors each year. The lights were born in 1907 without tremendous fanfare; they were simply tools to guide vessels safely in and out of the St. Joseph harbor, furthering commerce and the viability of the port.

Along the way, something changed in the way they were viewed. The lighthouses unintentionally became the backdrop for family weekends at the beach, days of fishing, and evening walks on the pier. In the process, they were woven into the collective consciousness of life on the Lake Michigan shoreline.

Today, the St. Joseph lighthouses are among the most beloved and photographed in Michigan. The sunset backdrops are magical. The red roof of the inner lighthouse is brilliant against bright blue skies. Images of the outer lighthouse cloaked in ice have received international acclaim on social media.

View 366 is a glimpse into the magic, the power, and the serenity surrounding the steel structures as depicted through 366 consecutive daily photos spanning one leap year. This story goes beyond what any one image or general collection of photos can tell. It connects the gradual and not-so-gradual daily shifts in weather. It shows the lighthouses as pivotal points that stand steadfast while the people, activities, and seasons evolve around them.

About the Project

The initial intent of photographing the lighthouses was not to take a full year of photos. That decision was made at the end of day three. It wasn't to create a book. That idea came months later. It started with the simple realization that the summer of 2011 was slipping away and I decided it would be nice to enjoy a few sunsets.

For three evenings in a row during late August, I went to Tiscornia Park on the north side of the St. Joseph lighthouses to photograph sunset.

As I returned to the car on the third day, I had the idea to photograph the lighthouses every day for one year. I wish I could say that there was some grand philosophical reason behind the concept beyond curiosity, but there wasn't. I didn't stop to consider the commitment it would become. I didn't think about how I would fit it around a full-time job and all the other things with which life is filled. There was no plan; I just decided to do it.

The guidelines I set for the project were simple:
    1) One or both of the lighthouses needed to be in each photo.
    2) I had to take photos every day for the entire year – without exception.

That was it. I could shoot any time of day. I could move from the north side of the pier to the south side of the pier and all the points in between. The lighthouses didn't need to be the focal point of the photos; one or both simply had to appear somewhere in the shot.

The idea for the book was brought up several months later by my mom when she was looking at some of the photos. She asked what I would do with them. I didn't have much of an answer, so she suggested assembling them into a book. In the end, I chose one photo from each day to represent my yearlong journey and that collection is *View 366*.

Day 149 – A Winter Tale
Saturday, January 21, 2012, 5:27 p.m.
Sunrise: 8:08 a.m.   Sunset: 5:46 p.m.

View366

A Year-long Visual Story of the St. Joseph Lighthouses

The St. Joseph lighthouses are touchstones for a community. They are a destination for the important moments of life – first dates, weddings, family gatherings, and senior portraits. They are a part of the ordinary moments as well. Their presence is an integral part of growing up and living in St. Joseph and southwest Michigan.

People connect with the lighthouses in a variety of ways – through fishing, boating, photography, sunset watching, kiteboarding, and simple walks on the piers. The setting is most active in the summer, but is often most interesting the other three seasons.

Although they've appeared in tens of thousands of photographs over the decades, the lighthouses can be new and interesting every day when you approach them with a quiet mind and openness to small surprises. Pushing beyond the thought that you've "seen it all" opens up a fresh scene every day. And that is true for anything in life.

I hope you enjoy this collection of photos and perspectives of the St. Joseph lighthouses. Through them, I offer you the opportunity to become acquainted with these familiar friends in a whole new way.

Laura Kraklau

Day 1 – Visual Intoxicant
Friday, August 26, 2011, 8:24 p.m.
Sunrise: 7:05 a.m.   Sunset: 8:30 p.m.

Sunset generates a creative adrenaline that tugs at your mind and pulls you back for another look. August 26, 2011, was the start of a year-long photographic connection to the daily world of the St. Joseph lighthouses. No one knew it at the time, though, including me.

Day 2 – Flight in Silhouette
Saturday, August 27, 2011, 8:20 p.m.
Sunrise: 7:06 a.m.   Sunset: 8:29 p.m.

Day 3 – Splash Zone
Sunday, August 28, 2011, 8:16 p.m.
Sunrise: 7:07 a.m.   Sunset: 8:27 p.m.

Three days of changes in the sky, the light, the water, and the people surrounding the lighthouses made me wonder how the incremental daily shifts through the seasons would play out over time. As I thought about that question, I decided to find out and photograph the St. Joseph icons every day for one year. In that moment, *View 366* was born.

Day 4 – Sun King

Monday, August 29, 2011, 8:19 p.m.
Sunrise: 7:08 a.m.   Sunset: 8:25 p.m.

Day 5 – Marks of Time

Tuesday, August 30, 2011, 7:49 p.m.
Sunrise: 7:09 a.m.   Sunset: 8:24 p.m.

Like notches on a kitchen doorframe that track a child's growth, the shades of weathered metal on the north pier are a record of the changes in Lake Michigan water levels.

Day 6 – Working Class Port
Wednesday, August 31, 2011, 7:35 p.m.
Sunrise: 7:10 a.m.   Sunset: 8:22 p.m.

Pleasure boating, sport fishing, and sailing define lake life in St. Joseph, yet that is only part of the story. The port has a long history of being a roll-up-your-sleeves-and-get-the-job-done kind of place where commercial vessels conduct commerce in the waterways around the lighthouses.

Day 7 – A Special Place on the Lake
Thursday, September 1, 2011, 4:12 p.m.
Sunrise: 7:11 a.m.   Sunset: 8:20 p.m.

Day 8 – Lazy Haze
Friday, September 2, 2011, 12:17 p.m.
Sunrise: 7:12 a.m.   Sunset: 8:19 p.m.

Day 10 – Traditions
Sunday, September 4, 2011, 10:39 a.m.
Sunrise: 7:14 a.m.   Sunset: 8:15 p.m.

The Tri-State Regatta is a Labor Day weekend tradition dating back to the 1940s. More than 100 sailboats arrive in St. Joseph during the early hours of Saturday for a one-day layover. They depart on the second leg of the Chicago-St. Joseph-Michigan City-Chicago race Sunday morning.

Day 9 – A Tourist's Perspective
Saturday, September 3, 2011, 11:16 a.m.
Sunrise: 7:13 a.m.   Sunset: 8:17 p.m.

Day 11 – A Knock on the Door

Monday, September 5, 2011, 8:26 a.m.
Sunrise: 7:15 a.m.   Sunset: 8:14 p.m.

Clear 53 degree air, a northwest wind whipping up a frothy mix, and the low morning sun were autumn's first calling card.

Day 12 – To Deeper Waters
Tuesday, September 6, 2011, 7:51 a.m.
Sunrise: 7:16 a.m.   Sunset: 8:12 p.m.

Day 13 – Candy Swirl
Wednesday, September 7, 2011, 8:10 p.m.
Sunrise: 7:17 a.m.   Sunset: 8:10 p.m.

Deep blue morning stillness is the sportsman's perfect playground,
while the gulls make twilight their own.

Day 15 – Guide the Way

Friday, September 9, 2011, 8:14 p.m.
Sunrise: 7:19 a.m.   Sunset: 8:07 p.m.

The Michigan ports of St. Joseph and Grand Haven boast the only two operational range light systems with intact catwalks and towers on the United States side of the Great Lakes.

Day 14 – Foreboding Currents

Thursday, September 8, 2011, 6:57 p.m.
Sunrise: 7:18 a.m.   Sunset: 8:08 p.m.

Day 16 – Quiet Tribute

Saturday, September 10, 2011, 7:48 p.m.
Sunrise: 7:20 a.m.   Sunset: 8:05 p.m.

While retrospectives and analysis dominated weekend television and online newsfeeds, nothing was a more inspiring 9/11 tenth anniversary tribute than a solitary sailboat flying the American flag.

Day 17 – Metallic Sheen
Sunday, September 11, 2011, 7:58 p.m.
Sunrise: 7:21 a.m.   Sunset: 8:03 p.m.

Day 18 – Grown-up Playground

Monday, September 12, 2011, 7:57 p.m.
Sunrise: 7:22 a.m.   Sunset: 8:01 p.m.

Wind, water, and large pieces of fabric…that is what Lake Michigan sports are made of.

Day 19 - Apocalyptic Sunset
Tuesday, September 13, 2011, 7:42 p.m.
Sunrise: 7:23 a.m.   Sunset: 8:00 p.m.

From first light, a smoldering scent and subtle haze hung in the air. It was from the Pagami
Creek wildfire near Ely, Minnesota. The smoke traveled more than 400 miles across
Wisconsin, Illinois, and Michigan to provide a faintly smoky sunset filter.

Day 20 – Molten Lava

Wednesday, September 14, 2011, 7:58 p.m.
Sunrise: 7:24 a.m.   Sunset: 7:58 p.m.

Heavy clouds dominated the sky, so it seemed likely we would be in for a gray close to the day.
Only the unobstructed view from the beach revealed a clear horizon and a remarkable sunset.

Day 21 – Crash
Thursday, September 15, 2011, 7:42 p.m.
Sunrise: 7:25 a.m.   Sunset: 7:56 p.m.

Day 22 – Scars of Time
Friday, September 16, 2011, 5:51 p.m.
Sunrise: 7:26 a.m.   Sunset: 7:54 p.m.

One drop of water does not cause steel to rust. One day of sunshine does not fade paint. It takes days and weeks that slowly fade into years to wear away at the polished exterior.

Day 24 – Morning Illumination
Sunday, September 18, 2011, 7:48 a.m.
Sunrise: 7:28 a.m.   Sunset: 7:51 p.m.

Day 23 – Beyond Reach
Saturday, September 17, 2011, 11:37 a.m.
Sunrise: 7:27 a.m.   Sunset: 7:53 p.m.

Day 25 – Ominous
Monday, September 19, 2011, 6:01 p.m.
Sunrise: 7:29 a.m.   Sunset: 7:49 p.m.

Day 26 – Beauty in Rituals

Tuesday, September 20, 2011, 7:44 a.m.
Sunrise: 7:31 a.m.   Sunset: 7:47 p.m.

The clatter from a fishing cart bumping across the seams in the concrete broke the morning silence. As the gentleman passed me on the pier, he offered a friendly morning greeting. His comfortable demeanor in the surroundings made it clear that this was a cherished ritual.

Day 27 – Pink Lemonade

Wednesday, September 21, 2011, 7:39 p.m.
Sunrise: 7:32 a.m.   Sunset: 7:46 p.m.

Day 28 – Mennonite Holiday

Thursday, September 22, 2011, 7:14 p.m.
Sunrise: 7:33 a.m.   Sunset: 7:44 p.m.

The young Mennonite women from Indiana were in town with their families.
Over several evenings, they walked on the pier, took sunset photos, and laughed as they dared the waves to spray them. Their joy was a reminder to not become numb to the wonders of the familiar lakefront setting.

Day 29 – Autumnal Equinox
Friday, September 23, 2011, 2:02 p.m.
Sunrise: 7:34 a.m.   Sunset: 7:42 p.m.

Day 30 – The Front Lines
Saturday, September 24, 2011, 4:07 p.m.
Sunrise: 7:35 a.m.   Sunset: 7:40 p.m.

Day 31 – Town in the Distance
Sunday, September 25, 2011, 3:57 p.m.
Sunrise: 7:36 a.m.   Sunset: 7:39 p.m.

On the sign: **Warning** — Structure is Not Designed for Public Access Proceed at Your Own Risk

Day 32 – In the Balance
Monday, September 26, 2011, 7:25 p.m.
Sunrise: 7:37 a.m.   Sunset: 7:37 p.m.

As days become more dark than light, the long walk into winter should come with its own "proceed at your own risk" warning.

Day 33 – Moon Tower

Tuesday, September 27, 2011, 8:11 p.m.
Sunrise: 7:38 a.m. **Sunset: 7:35 p.m.**

Although the Fresnel lens was still housed in the inner lighthouse, it was no longer used. A beacon attached to the railing handled the job of nighttime illumination.

Day 35 – Gaining Momentum

Thursday, September 29, 2011, 6:58 p.m.
Sunrise: 7:40 a.m. **Sunset: 7:32 p.m.**

Thursday evening, the wind began to pick up –
a foreshadowing of the weather to come the next day.

Day 34 – Standing Tall

Wednesday, September 28, 2011, 7:14 p.m.
Sunrise: 7:39 a.m. **Sunset: 7:33 p.m.**

Day 36 – Fury

Friday, September 30, 2011, 4:05 p.m.
Sunrise: 7:41 a.m.   Sunset: 7:30 p.m.

The lure of a spectacular water show outweighed the punishment served up by the northwest wind. Thrill seekers gathered at the beach to watch pure power unleashed.

Day 37 – Shadow Art

Saturday, October 1, 2011, 3:28 p.m.
Sunrise: 7:42 a.m.   Sunset: 7:28 p.m.

The wind of the previous day created a clean sand canvas for long afternoon shadows.

Day 38 – Emergence

Sunday, October 2, 2011, 7:26 p.m.
Sunrise: 7:44 a.m.   Sunset: 7:26 p.m.

After three days, bluster turned into serenity.

Day 39 – Geometric Expression

Monday, October 3, 2011, 7:11 p.m.
Sunrise: 7:45 a.m.   Sunset: 7:25 p.m.

Day 40 – Glow

Tuesday, October 4, 2011, 7:19 p.m.
Sunrise: 7:46 a.m.   Sunset: 7:23 p.m.

Day 41 – Waiting for the Bell to Ring

Wednesday, October 5, 2011, 7:06 p.m.
Sunrise: 7:47 a.m.   Sunset: 7:21 p.m.

Fishermen use holes in the pier to anchor their fishing poles while they wait for a bite. Some use a small bell at the end of the pole to alert them that the catch of the day is on the line.

Day 42 – Metal Art: New and Vintage

Thursday, October 6, 2011, 12:16 p.m.
Sunrise: 7:48 a.m.   Sunset: 7:20 p.m.

Art can be an intentional expression that demonstrates the creator's vision. Then there are those creations, like the lighthouses, that don't begin as art, but become cherished like museum pieces because they endure the test of time.

Day 43 – Sail On, Autumn Night
Friday, October 7, 2011, 7:06 p.m.
Sunrise: 7:49 a.m.   Sunset: 7:18 p.m.

Day 44 – Beach Day

Saturday, October 8, 2011, 4:04 p.m.
Sunrise: 7:50 a.m.   Sunset: 7:16 p.m.

Silver Beach was once the site of an amusement park famous throughout the Midwest. The buildings, rides, and games have been gone for nearly 40 years but the beach still is considered one of the best on Lake Michigan.

Day 45 – Bowing to the Light

Sunday, October 9, 2011, 7:04 p.m.
Sunrise: 7:51 a.m.   Sunset: 7:15 p.m.

Day 46 – No Warm Night Wasted
Monday, October 10, 2011, 6:45 p.m.
Sunrise: 7:52 a.m.   Sunset: 7:13 p.m.

An 80 degree day in October is rare; several in a row had
the power to make us all forget it was autumn. Local sailors
graciously accepted the warm gift.

Day 47 – Seasonal Blend

Tuesday, October 11, 2011, 1:01 p.m.
Sunrise: 7:53 a.m.   Sunset: 7:11 p.m.

For a few moments, the unseasonable heat, the angle of the sun, and the absence of
wind made the perfect conditions for the sky and water to blend as one.

Day 48 – Good Morning, Moon
Wednesday, October 12, 2011, 8:05 a.m.
Sunrise: 7:54 a.m.   Sunset: 7:10 p.m.

Day 49 – Up
Thursday, October 13, 2011, 2:03 p.m.
Sunrise: 7:56 a.m.   Sunset: 7:08 p.m.

Day 50 – Restless Autumn
Friday, October 14, 2011, 9:44 a.m.
Sunrise: 7:57 a.m.   Sunset: 7:07 p.m.

Day 51 – Wind Pilots

Saturday, October 15, 2011, 10:19 a.m.
Sunrise: 7:58 a.m.   Sunset: 7:05 p.m.

Too windy for boating
Too wavy for walking on the pier
Just right for playing in the air currents.

Day 52 – Weather Worn

Sunday, October 16, 2011, 4:11 p.m.
Sunrise: 7:59 a.m.   Sunset: 7:03 p.m.

Day 53 – Love Letters

Monday, October 17, 2011, 5:48 p.m.
Sunrise: 8:00 a.m.   Sunset: 7:02 p.m.

Simple expressions of love say the most. Here's to the Ryans and Sarahs of the world.

Day 54 – Up Close
Tuesday, October 18, 2011, 12:31 p.m.
Sunrise: 8:01 a.m.   Sunset: 7:00 p.m.

Day 55 – No Admittance
Wednesday, October 19, 2011, 5:50 p.m.
Sunrise: 8:02 a.m.   Sunset: 6:59 p.m.

Within 36 hours, the base of the outer light went from safe to engulfed. The Coast Guard estimated that waves reached heights of 10 feet. The unusually stormy fall created problems for freighters accessing the channel later in the year.

Day 56 – Rave On
Thursday, October 20, 2011, 12:20 p.m.
Sunrise: 8:04 a.m.   Sunset: 6:57 p.m.

Day 57 – Deep Breath
Friday, October 21, 2011, 6:42 p.m.
Sunrise: 8:05 a.m.   Sunset: 6:56 p.m.

Day 58 – Profile
Saturday, October 22, 2011, 3:46 p.m.
Sunrise: 8:06 a.m.   Sunset: 6:54 p.m.

Day 59 – Pointing to Where Dreams Live

Sunday, October 23, 2011, 4:10 p.m.
Sunrise: 8:07 a.m.   Sunset: 6:53 p.m.

Day 60 – Century Companions
Monday, October 24, 2011, 6:17 p.m.
Sunrise: 8:08 a.m.   Sunset: 6:51 p.m.

At the beginning of the 20th century, investments were made in St. Joseph's transportation infrastructure. The lighthouses and railroad swing bridge over the St. Joseph River were built within a few years of each other – the bridge in 1904 and the lighthouses in 1907. More than 100 years later, they still stand strong together.

Day 61 – Morning Run
Tuesday, October 25, 2011, 8:42 a.m.
Sunrise: 8:10 a.m.   Sunset: 6:50 p.m.

Day 62 – Dedication
Wednesday, October 26, 2011, 11:44 a.m.
Sunrise: 8:11 a.m.   Sunset: 6:48 p.m.

I didn't expect to see anyone out on such a gloomy day, yet one man stood in the drizzle and wind. It was hard to tell if he was there for the fishing or for the thinking.

Day 63 – Sky Art

Thursday, October 27, 2011, 6:12 p.m.
Sunrise: 8:12 a.m.   Sunset: 6:47 p.m.

Day 64 – Summer Echoes

Friday, October 28, 2011, 4:33 p.m.
Sunrise: 8:13 a.m.   Sunset: 6:46 p.m.

Quiet beach. Empty lake. Lifeguards were just a memory.

Day 65 – No Cares
Saturday, October 29, 2011, 2:49 p.m.
Sunrise: 8:14 a.m.   Sunset: 6:45 p.m.

To soar is to separate from worry.

41

Day 66 – Sunday Stroll
Sunday, October 30, 2011, 9:44 a.m.
Sunrise: 8:16 a.m.   Sunset: 6:43 p.m.

Day 67 – All Hallow's Eve
Monday, October 31, 2011, 6:13 p.m.
Sunrise: 8:17 a.m.   Sunset: 6:42 p.m.

Day 68 – Tipped in Gold

Tuesday, November 1, 2011, 5:39 p.m.
Sunrise: 8:18 a.m.   Sunset: 6:40 p.m.

Day 69 – Evidence of Life

Wednesday, November 2, 2011, 5:46 p.m.
Sunrise: 8:19 a.m.   Sunset: 6:39 p.m.

When out-of-town visitors leave, there is an active community of locals drawn to the energy of the lake. Warmth isn't the prerequisite for being here. The uniqueness of each season is the lure.

Day 70 – Overspill
Thursday, November 3, 2011, 11:34 a.m.
Sunrise: 8:20 a.m.   Sunset: 6:38 p.m.

Day 71 – Watercolors
Friday, November 4, 2011, 6:37 p.m.
Sunrise: 8:22 a.m.   Sunset: 6:37 p.m.

Nature creates what artists can only loosely translate.

Day 72 – Fish While They're Biting
Saturday, November 5, 2011, 1:44 p.m.
Sunrise: 8:23 a.m.   Sunset: 6:35 p.m.

Throughout the year, those who fished from the pier seemed content to talk with the person next to them, listen to the game on a portable radio, or simply get lost in thought while waiting for a bite. While most probably had a phone tucked away in a pocket, they chose to spend the time mostly unencumbered by technology.

Day 73 – Wind Catcher

Sunday, November 6, 2011, 3:25 p.m.
Sunrise: 7:24 a.m.   Sunset: 5:34 p.m.

A solid south wind was the open invitation kiteboarders needed to skim through the empty waters along the north side of the pier.

Day 75 – PermaCloud
Tuesday, November 8, 2011, 12:20 p.m.
Sunrise: 7:27 a.m.   Sunset: 5:32 p.m.

Day 74 – Dark Days
Monday, November 7, 2011, 4:55 p.m.
Sunrise: 7:25 a.m.   Sunset: 5:33 p.m.

Day 76 – Driven

Wednesday, November 9, 2011, 12:30 p.m.
Sunrise: 7:28 a.m.   Sunset: 5:31 p.m.

Wind direction is a key factor in how water and the piers interact.
This day, the driving south wind created an ethereal mist that rose from the channel.

Day 77 – Hole in the Sky

Thursday, November 10, 2011, 5:07 p.m.
Sunrise: 7:29 a.m.   Sunset: 5:30 p.m.

Day 78 – Golden Grasses

Friday, November 11, 2011, 5:14 p.m.
Sunrise: 7:30 a.m.   Sunset: 5:29 p.m.

Day 79 – Fishing Lair

Saturday, November 12, 2011, 3:24 p.m.
Sunrise: 7:32 a.m.   Sunset: 5:28 p.m.

He fished alone. It was clear he wanted it that way. Once he got wise to my photo taking, he shot a cantankerous look over his shoulder.

Day 80 – Solo Sunset Flight

Sunday, November 13, 2011, 5:22 p.m.
Sunrise: 7:33 a.m.   Sunset: 5:27 p.m.

Favorable weather gave kiteboarders another chance to coax a little more fun out of the lake before winter.

Day 81 – Brushstrokes

Monday, November 14, 2011, 11:14 A.M.
Sunrise: 7:34 a.m.   Sunset: 5:26 p.m.

Under the endless tarp of textured clouds there was a sense that the path ahead led to where possibilities begin.

Day 82 – Love Will Tear Us Apart

Tuesday, November 15, 2011, 4:53 p.m.
Sunrise: 7:35 a.m.   Sunset: 5:25 p.m.

Look carefully and you'll see where someone scribed the post-punk
message of angst "Love Will Tear Us Apart" onto the outer lighthouse.

Day 83 – Sherbet Sunrise
Wednesday, November 16, 2011, 8:08 a.m.
Sunrise: 7:36 a.m.   Sunset: 5:24 p.m.

Day 84 – Water Rage
Thursday, November 17, 2011, 4:40 p.m.
Sunrise: 7:38 a.m.   Sunset: 5:24 p.m.

Like a giant claw coming up from the lake, the water made a menacing
move toward the outer lighthouse. The lighthouse won.

Day 85 – Endless Summer
Friday, November 18, 2011, 5:29 p.m.
Sunrise: 7:39 a.m.   Sunset: 5:23 p.m.

Real surfers surf Lake Michigan... in November.

Day 86 – Sign of the Season
Saturday, November 19, 2011, 4:06 p.m.
Sunrise: 7:40 a.m.   Sunset: 5:22 p.m.

Day 87 – November Haunting
Sunday, November 20, 2011, 4:58 p.m.
Sunrise: 7:41 a.m.   Sunset: 5:21 p.m.

Only weeks before, the sound of people filled the air and brightness opened a vibrant sky.
Then November gloom crept around the edges of the pier. With it came a haunting loneliness.

Day 88 – Life in the Moment
Monday, November 21, 2011, 4:47 p.m.
Sunrise: 7:43 a.m.   Sunset: 5:21 p.m.

Day 89 – During Storms or High Seas
Tuesday, November 22, 2011, 12:55 p.m.
Sunrise: 7:44 a.m.   Sunset: 5:20 p.m.

Limited scenic options focused attention on an easily ignored sign that had clearly been on the railing of the south pier for many years.

Day 90 – Built on a Rock
Wednesday, November 23, 2011, 4:31 p.m.
Sunrise: 7:45 a.m.   Sunset: 5:19 p.m.

Chipped concrete at the base of the inner lighthouse and rust streaks on the tower tell the story of time.

Day 91 – Air Patrol
Thursday, November 24, 2011, 4:06 p.m.
Sunrise: 7:46 a.m   Sunset: 5:19 p.m.

Day 92 – Line Up

Friday, November 25, 2011, 1:41 p.m.
Sunrise: 7:47 a.m.   Sunset: 5:18 p.m.

"The piers have served an unexpected purpose. From early dawn until late at night scores of dangling lines held by patient fisherman may be seen." *History of St. Joseph*, L. Benj. Reber, 1925.

Day 93 – Placid
Saturday, November 26, 2011, 11:17 a.m.
Sunrise: 7:48 a.m.   Sunset: 5:18 p.m.

Day 94 – Turbulence
Sunday, November 27, 2011, 2:07 p.m.
Sunrise: 7:49 a.m.   Sunset: 5:17 p.m.

A sleeping cat became a seething monster overnight.

Day 95 – Frosted Hiding Place

Monday, November 28, 2011, 1:35 p.m.
Sunrise: 7:51 a.m.   Sunset: 5:17 p.m.

The original inner light Fresnel lens spent its final November encased in its protective perch. On October 4, 2012, the United States Coast Guard retired it for LED technology. Marquette-based Superior Lighthouse Restorations removed the light for restoration and eventual display.

Day 96 – Plume

Tuesday, November 29, 2011, 12:54 p.m.
Sunrise: 7:52 a.m.   Sunset: 5:16 p.m.

Day 97 – Running Waves
Wednesday, November 30, 2011, 4:48 p.m.
Sunrise: 7:53 a.m.   Sunset: 5:16 p.m

Day 98 – Top Gun
Thursday, December 1, 2011, 4:49 p.m.
Sunrise: 7:54 a.m.   Sunset: 5:16 p.m.

All was quiet except for the small plane performing a flyby of the lights.

Day 99 – Harmony
Friday, December 2, 2011, 5:03 p.m.
Sunrise: 7:55 a.m.   Sunset: 5:15 p.m.

Day 100 – Slipping Southward

Saturday, December 3, 2011, 4:54 p.m.
Sunrise: 7:56 a.m.   Sunset: 5:15 p.m.

When the winter sun sets far to the south, a long walk north along the beach is what it takes to bring the lighthouses and sunset together in the same frame.

Day 101 – Somber Musings
Sunday, December 4, 2011, 4:12 p.m.
Sunrise: 7:57 a.m.   Sunset: 5:15 p.m.

Day 103 – Waiting
Tuesday, December 6, 2011, 5:00 p.m.
Sunrise: 7:59 a.m.   Sunset: 5:15 p.m.

After running aground in shallow waters 500 feet off the pier heads, the Manitowac waited on the horizon for the Coast Guard to inspect it for damage. Weighed down by its 12,500 ton cargo of limestone, the freighter had managed to rock free from a buildup of silt caused by unusually strong autumn winds. The incident raised concern about the future of commercial shipping in the absence of federal dredging dollars.

Day 102 – Simple Day
Monday, December 5, 2011, 1:18 p.m.
Sunrise: 7:58 a.m.   Sunset: 5:15 p.m.

Day 104 – Symphony in Pink

Wednesday, December 7, 2011, 5:12 p.m.
Sunrise: 8:00 a.m.   Sunset: 5:15 p.m.

Winter sunsets bathe us in subtlety.

Day 106 – Begin the Beginning
Friday, December 9, 2011, 11:37 a.m.
Sunrise: 8:02 a.m.   Sunset: 5:15 p.m.

The uncertainty of the future obscures recognition of the final snowfall as it happens.
The first snow of the season is evident in the moment.

Day 105 – So Far Away
Thursday, December 8, 2011, 5:02 p.m.
Sunrise: 8:01 a.m.   Sunset: 5:15 p.m.

Day 107 – Blue Chill
Saturday, December 10, 2011, 3:59 p.m.
Sunrise: 8:03 a.m.   Sunset: 5:15 p.m.

Day 108 – Murmur Through the Trees
Sunday, December 11, 2011, 2:41 p.m.
Sunrise: 8:03 a.m.   Sunset: 5:15 p.m.

Day 109 – Field of Gold
Monday, December 12, 2011, 11:23 a.m.
Sunrise: 8:04 a.m.   Sunset: 5:15 p.m.

Day 110 – Silver Morning
Tuesday, December 13, 2011, 9:03 a.m.
Sunrise: 8:05 a.m.   Sunset: 5:15 p.m.

Day 112 – Wicked
Thursday, December 15, 2011, 12:33 p.m.
Sunrise: 8:06 a.m.   Sunset: 5:15 p.m.

Day 111 – Quiet Hibernation
Wednesday, December 14, 2011, 12:06 p.m.
Sunrise: 8:06 a.m.   Sunset: 5:15 p.m.

Day 113 – Coast Guard Cruise
Friday, December 16, 2011, 3:36 p.m.
Sunrise: 8:07 a.m.   Sunset: 5:16 p.m.

The Coast Guard station in St. Joseph is just up river from the lighthouses. Established in 1874, the station patrols approximately 850 square miles of Lake Michigan, and enforces the security zones for two nuclear power plants.

Day 114 – No Excuses

Saturday, December 17, 2011, 2:07 p.m.
Sunrise: 8:08 a.m.   Sunset: 5:16 p.m.

Good fishing won out over bad weather. The next day, the elements were just a memory.

Day 115 – Perfectly Framed

Sunday, December 18, 2011, 12:59 p.m.
Sunrise: 8:09 a.m.   Sunset: 5:16 p.m.

Day 116 – Through the Cat's Eye

Monday, December 19, 2011, 1:16 p.m.
Sunrise: 8:09 a.m.   Sunset: 5:17 p.m.

A small dune at the end of the catwalk provided the elevation
needed for a new perspective on the lighthouse.

Day 118 – Distant Lights
Wednesday, December 21, 2011, 4:55 p.m.
Sunrise: 8:10 a.m.   Sunset: 5:18 p.m.

Day 119 – Winter Solstice
Thursday, December 22, 2011, 2:37 p.m.
Sunrise: 8:11 a.m.   Sunset: 5:18 p.m.

Some see the first day of winter as a dive into darkness.
Others optimistically view it as the start of the journey back toward the sun.

Day 117 – Stripped Down
Tuesday, December 20, 2011, 12:19 p.m.
Sunrise: 8:10 a.m.   Sunset: 5:17 p.m.

Day 120 – Dressed in Red

Friday, December 23, 2011, 2:31 p.m.
Sunrise: 8:11 a.m.   Sunset: 5:19 p.m.

Was that Santa fishing on the pier before his big day?

Day 121 – Christmas Eve Trek

Saturday, December 24, 2011, 2:14 p.m.
Sunrise: 8:12 a.m.   Sunset: 5:19 p.m.

Mild weather and sunshine during the frenzied Christmas holiday brought an opportunity for people to focus on the simple pleasures of family and nature.

Day 122 – The Yule Tide

Sunday, December 25, 2011, 10:54 a.m.
Sunrise: 8:12 a.m.   Sunset: 5:20 p.m.

Day 123 – Sugar Soft Sand

Monday, December 26, 2011, 3:14 p.m.
Sunrise: 8:12 a.m.   Sunset: 5:20 p.m.

The wind can be a blunt instrument shaping clumsy outcomes. At other times, it can
sculpt the tiniest of particles into perfect patterns with unfailing precision.

Day 124 – And…Action!
Tuesday, December 27, 2011, 2:19 p.m.
Sunrise: 8:13 a.m.   Sunset: 5:21 p.m.

A video crew from New York shot footage of the lighthouses with
waves providing the action.

Day 125 – Risky
Wednesday, December 28, 2011, 1:43 p.m.
Sunrise: 8:13 a.m.   Sunset: 5:22 p.m.

A group of us on the beach watched while the cyclist rode up the icy
pier and propped his bike against the base of the inner lighthouse.
He walked the narrow concrete strip on the side of the lighthouse
and proceeded to kneel on the thin layer of ice. He leaned over and
appeared to scoop water from the rushing waves with his helmet.

Day 126 – Fishermen's Row
Thursday, December 29, 2011, 12:14 p.m.
Sunrise: 8:13 a.m.   Sunset: 5:23 p.m.

Day 127 – Whitefish Biting
Friday, December 30, 2011, 11:00 a.m.
Sunrise: 8:13 a.m.   Sunset: 5:23 p.m.

Open water made angling for whitefish an attractive late-season proposition for those willing to brave the chill in the air.

Day 128 – Majestic Deception
Saturday, December 31, 2011, 4:18 p.m.
Sunrise: 8:14 a.m.   Sunset: 5:24 p.m.

The year ended with unexpected calm, with little hint of what would come next.

Day 129 – In with a Bang
Sunday, January 1, 2012, 12:29 p.m.
Sunrise: 8:14 a.m.   Sunset: 5:25 p.m.
Within 20 short hours, lake conditions drastically changed.

Day 130 – Relentless Rage

Monday, January 2, 2012, 2:56 p.m.
Sunrise: 8:14 a.m.   Sunset: 5:26 p.m.

Repeated explosions of frigid water cast an icy mold that
shrouded the lighthouse's true identity.

Day 131 – Return to Calm

Tuesday, January 3, 2012, 5:08 p.m.
Sunrise: 8:14 a.m.   Sunset: 5:27 p.m.

After two days of relentless pounding by the surf, the
lighthouses were granted a reprieve from the abuse.

77

Day 132 – Powdered Sugar Icing
Wednesday, January 4, 2012, 12:37 p.m.
Sunrise: 8:14 a.m.   Sunset: 5:28 p.m.

By the fourth day of the New Year, we began to experience the yo-yo weather patterns that would dominate the winter of 2012. Blustery cold bursts were followed by strings of warm days. Consequently, the typical buildup of ice on the lake, pier, and outer lighthouse never took hold.

Day 133 – Ice Castle
Thursday, January 5, 2012, 12:31 p.m.
Sunrise: 8:14 a.m.　　　Sunset: 5:29 p.m.
Only icy remnants remained of the tumultuous weather that battered the structures on the pier a few days earlier.

Day 134 – Aztec Warrior

Friday, January 6, 2012, 5:20 p.m.
Sunrise: 8:14 a.m.   **Sunset: 5:30 p.m.**

With his headdress stretched to the heavens and his hand outreached above the setting sun,
the Aztec Warrior blessed the night that was about to begin.

Day 135 – News of the Day

Saturday, January 7, 2012, 5:24 p.m.
Sunrise: 8:14 a.m.   **Sunset: 5:31 p.m.**

Day 137 – Winter...with a Twist

Monday, January 9, 2012, 5:17 p.m.
Sunrise: 8:13 a.m.   **Sunset: 5:33 p.m.**

Day 136 – Open Up and Say "Ah"

Sunday, January 8, 2012, 1:38 p.m.
Sunrise: 8:14 a.m.   **Sunset: 5:32 p.m.**

Unseasonably mild temperatures and calm weather created the right opportunity to put $99,000 in emergency federal funding to work for a rare winter dredging. The unusual timing for this work was necessary to re-open the shipping channel closed by a build up of silt from the strong autumn winds.

Day 138 – So Big, So Small

Tuesday, January 10, 2012, 5:30 p.m.
Sunrise: 8:13 a.m.   Sunset: 5:34 p.m.

Man, man's best friend, and man's creation.

Day 139 – The Winter That Wasn't
Wednesday, January 11, 2012, 5:39 p.m.
Sunrise: 8:13 a.m.   Sunset: 5:35 p.m.

Wool winter coats were left at home in favor of sweatshirts for a comfortable sunset beach walk on a beautifully warm January night.

Day 140 – Transition

Thursday, January 12, 2012, 11:02 a.m.
Sunrise: 8:13 a.m.   Sunset: 5:36 p.m.

The glow of sunny days and rich sunsets drained away as rougher weather approached.

Day 141 – Witch's Brew

Friday, January 13, 2012, 11:30 a.m.
Sunrise: 8:12 a.m.   Sunset: 5:37 p.m.

The lake bubbled and frothed like a cauldron of mystical potion.

Day 142 – Crystal Cloak
Saturday, January 14, 2012, 3:25 p.m.
Sunrise: 8:12 a.m.   Sunset: 5:38 p.m.

Fresh snow sparkled. Gray skies approached.
The loneliness of winter hung in the air.

Day 143 – Through the Dunes
Sunday, January 15, 2012, 2:23 p.m.
Sunrise: 8:11 a.m.   Sunset: 5:39 p.m.

Remnants of summer's bountiful greenery stood void of life,
resting, waiting, for the resurrection spring would bring.

Day 144 – Vanishing Act
Monday, January 16, 2012, 10:37 a.m.
Sunrise: 8:11 a.m.   Sunset: 5:40 p.m.

The golden magician cast a spell over the telltale signs of winter, making the icy remnants fade in the warmth of his rays.

Day 145 – Uncertainty
Tuesday, January 17, 2012, 12:14 p.m.
Sunrise: 8:10 a.m.   Sunset: 5:42 p.m.

Day 146 – Subtle Shades of Gray
Wednesday, January 18, 2012, 12:36 p.m.
Sunrise: 8:10 a.m.   Sunset: 5:43 p.m.

As if playing a part in the artist's fantasy, sky and water wore matching
gray-green hues to create a reality that felt like a painting.

Day 147 – Over the Top
Thursday, January 19, 2012, 11:56 a.m.
Sunrise: 8:09 a.m.   Sunset: 5:44 p.m.

Day 148 – Small Boat, Big Adventure
Friday, January 20, 2012, 9:30 a.m.
Sunrise: 8:09 a.m.   Sunset: 5:45 p.m.

Even in winter, the Coast Guard conducts rescue drills and keeps a close eye on the piers.

Day 149 – A Winter Story

Saturday, January 21, 2012, 11:48 a.m.
Sunrise: 8:08 a.m.   Sunset: 5:46 p.m.

Ice buildup along the shore extended its reach into the lake as waves lapped at the edges.

Day 150 – The Coldest Winter Chill
Sunday, January 22, 2012, 2:16 p.m.
Sunrise: 8:07 a.m.   Sunset: 5:48 p.m.

Day 151 – Gray Wind Blowing
Monday, January 23, 2012, 1:54 p.m.
Sunrise: 8:07 a.m.   Sunset: 5:49 p.m.

Day 152 – On the Rocks
Tuesday, January 24, 2012, 11:57 a.m.
Sunrise: 8:06 a.m.   Sunset: 5:50 p.m.

Despite sunless days, the landscape around the lighthouses changed considerably. Sunday's healthy coating of pier ice dissolved into little more than cold remnants over the next two days.

Day 153 – Midday Visit
Wednesday, January 25, 2012, 11:54 a.m.
Sunrise: 8:05 a.m.   Sunset: 5:51 p.m.

A late-in-the-season shipment of road salt, concrete, or other essential material waited offshore for its time to move into port.

Day 154 – Fridged
Thursday, January 26, 2012, 1:50 p.m.
Sunrise: 8:04 a.m.   Sunset: 5:53 p.m.

Day 155 – Open Waters
Friday, January 27, 2012, 5:21 p.m.
Sunrise: 8:04 a.m.   Sunset: 5:54 p.m.

Typically in January, the lighthouses are surrounded by shifting ice.
This winter's unusual warmth left open waters most of the season.

Day 156 – Impact
Saturday, January 28, 2012, 5:39 p.m.
Sunrise: 8:03 a.m.   Sunset: 5:55 p.m.

The struggle between the power of the lake and the strength of the lighthouses
has played out for decades without resolution.

Day 157 – Cotton Candy Sunset
Sunday, January 29, 2012, 5:47 p.m.
Sunrise: 8:02 a.m.   Sunset: 5:57 p.m.

Nothing breaks the back of dreary winter days

Day 158 – Fleece

Monday, January 30, 2012, 5:07 p.m.
Sunrise: 8:01 a.m.   Sunset: 5:58 p.m.

Sometimes only a downy canopy separates Earth from the rest of the universe.

Day 159 – Climate Change
Tuesday, January 31, 2012, 5:36 p.m.
Sunrise: 8:00 a.m.   Sunset: 5:59 p.m.

A winter void of significant snow and dotted with days well above freezing left many to wonder about what climate change might mean for us.

Day 160 – Angler on Alert
Wednesday, February 1, 2012, 5:13 p.m.
Sunrise: 7:59 a.m.   Sunset: 6:00 p.m.

The man watched over his lines anchored in the sand. He must have felt the camera's presence because he would occasionally look over his shoulder then quickly turn his focus back to his lines floating in the water.

Day 161 – Washed Ashore

Thursday, February 2, 2012, 4:57 p.m.
Sunrise: 7:58 a.m.   Sunset: 6:02 p.m.

Rough waters tossed a wave-worn remnant of a tree onto the beach. It remained a fixture for many weeks.

Day 162 – Sky Meets Water

Friday, February 3, 2012, 5:37 p.m.
Sunrise: 7:57 a.m.   Sunset: 6:03 p.m.

Day 163 – Tie-dye Sky
Saturday, February 4, 2012, 5:50 p.m.
Sunrise: 7:56 a.m.   Sunset: 6:04 p.m.

Day 164 – Lazy Morning Fog

Sunday, February 5, 2012, 9:45 a.m.
Sunrise: 7:55 a.m.   Sunset: 6:06 p.m.

The lighthouses stood silently wrapped in a muslin veil that allowed the morning sun to softly illuminate their faces.

Day 165 – Faith
Monday, February 6, 2012, 5:39 p.m.
Sunrise: 7:54 a.m.   Sunset: 6:07 p.m.

Faith is the belief in things not seen; it is what keeps summer alive during the grayest winter days.

Day 166 – Winter Lake Blue
Tuesday, February 7, 2012, 5:42 p.m.
Sunrise: 7:52 a.m.   Sunset: 6:08 p.m.

Somewhere between violet and green lies winter lake blue with all its subtleties of strength, serenity, and emotion.

Day 167 – Magenta Swirl
Wednesday, February 8, 2012, 6:20 p.m.
Sunrise: 7:51 a.m.   Sunset: 6:09 p.m.

Day 168 – Essence
Thursday, February 9, 2012, 5:57 p.m.
Sunrise: 7:50 a.m.   Sunset: 6:11 p.m.

The essence of a mood is found in dreamy soft focus.

Day 169 – Change in the Weather
Friday, February 10, 2012, 11:42 a.m.
Sunrise: 7:49 a.m.   Sunset: 6:12 p.m.

If change had a color...

Day 170 – The Lake Effect
Saturday, February 11, 2012, 3:27 p.m.
Sunrise: 7:47 a.m.   **Sunset: 6:13 p.m.**

Weeks of unusually warm days lulled southwest Michigan into a false sense of season. Then, 16 inches of lake effect snow brought us back to reality.

Day 171 – Ice Lines
Sunday, February 12, 2012, 10:37 a.m.
Sunrise: 7:46 a.m.   **Sunset: 6:15 p.m.**

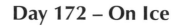

Day 172 – On Ice

Monday, February 13, 2012, 12:55 p.m.
Sunrise: 7:45 a.m.   Sunset: 6:16 p.m.

Winter provides a daily shift in the appearance of the pier and its surroundings, from where snow is positioned on the lighthouse roof to how the ice is layered on the catwalk. The incremental changes create a unique energy worth exploring every day.

Day 173 – Bird Watching

Tuesday, February 14, 2012, 9:38 a.m.
Sunrise: 7:44 a.m.   Sunset: 6:17 p.m.

There is a community of avid birdwatchers who come to the lake at all times of the year. Migratory patterns bring a variety of ducks, terns, gulls, and even the occasional snow owl to the beach. On this morning, one of those birdwatchers braved the cold and icy walk to the end of the pier to see what feathered friends were visiting.

Day 174 – Cocoa Marshmallow Fluff

Wednesday, February 15, 2012, 5:36 p.m.
Sunrise: 7:43 a.m.   Sunset: 6:19 p.m.

The sand and snow blended in a way that looked less like dirty snow and more like cocoa powder sprinkled onto marshmallow fluff.

Day 175 – Sunset Serenity

Thursday, February 16, 2012, 6:22 p.m.
Sunrise: 7:41 a.m.   Sunset: 6:20 p.m.

Day 176 – Where the Clouds End

Friday, February 17, 2012, 5:32 p.m.
Sunrise: 7:39 a.m.   Sunset: 6:21 p.m.

Day 177 – Frothy

Saturday, February 18, 2012, 2:37 p.m.
Sunrise: 7:38 a.m.   Sunset: 6:22 p.m.

Day 178 – Empty Arms

Sunday, February 19, 2012, 4:47 p.m.
Sunrise: 7:37 a.m.   Sunset: 6:23 p.m.

Empty arms stretch to the sky,
A call on heaven for warmth and summer breezes.
A lonely existance on the water,
Waiting for the swirl of life to return.

Day 179 – Etched on the Sky

Monday, February 20, 2012, 5:52 p.m.
Sunrise: 7:35 a.m.   Sunset: 6:25 p.m.

Day 180 – False Horizon
Tuesday, February 21, 2012, 6:19 p.m.
Sunrise: 7:34 a.m.   Sunset: 6:26 p.m.

Clouds in the west forced an early sunset.

Day 181 – A Lesson in Fishing

Wednesday, February 22, 2012, 12:53 p.m.
Sunrise: 7:32 a.m.   Sunset: 6:27 p.m.

Old Man Winter's absence continued to be felt when one would expect the lighthouses to be in the throes of bluster and cold. It gave this man many opportunities to bring his puppy to the pier and teach him the finer points of fishing.

NO
LIFEGUARD ON DUTY,
SWIM AT YOUR OWN RISK,
DEEP WATER,
STRONG CURRENT.

NO
LAUNCHING
OF MOTORIZED
PERSONAL
WATERCRAFT
FROM THIS
PARK
VIOLATERS
WILL BE
TICKETED

Day 182 – Warnings and Consequences

Thursday, February 23, 2012, 11:51 a.m.
Sunrise: 7:31 a.m.   Sunset: 6:28 p.m.

A list of rules made by man and nature carries some harsh penalties
– expressed and implied.

Day 183 – Another Dusting
Friday, February 24, 2012, 5:10 p.m.
Sunrise: 7:29 a.m.   Sunset: 6:30 p.m.

Day 184 – The Gathering
Saturday, February 25, 2012, 3:40 p.m.
Sunrise: 7:28 a.m.   Sunset: 6:31 p.m.

Day 185 – One Drop

Sunday, February 26, 2012, 11:49 a.m.
Sunrise: 7:26 a.m.   Sunset: 6:32 p.m.

From a seat on the frigid concrete came a new perspective through
icicles that hung from the railing and slowly melted in the sun.

Day 186 – Mystery's Mood
Monday, February 27, 2012, 6:28 p.m.
Sunrise: 7:25 a.m.   Sunset: 6:33 p.m.

Day 187 – Big Sky Water
Tuesday, February 28, 2012, 12:43 p.m.
Sunrise: 7:23 a.m.   Sunset: 6:34 p.m.
The day opened its arms wide and showed how vast the universe is.

Day 188 – Halo: Leap 366

Wednesday, February 29, 2012, 5:38 p.m.
Sunrise: 7:21 a.m.   Sunset: 6:36 p.m.

On a day that comes along once every four years, the thick clouds cleared for just moment.

Day 190 – Midday Beacon

Friday, March 2, 2012, 1:14 p.m.
Sunrise: 7:18 a.m.   Sunset: 6:38 p.m.

Day 189 – Misty Dream

Thursday, March 1, 2012, 5:37 p.m.
Sunrise: 7:20 a.m.   Sunset: 6:37 p.m.

On a long and lonely afternoon, gray was the color of the day.

Day 191 – March is a Lion
Saturday, March 3, 2012, 12:06 p.m.
Sunrise: 7:17 a.m.   Sunset: 6:39 p.m.

There is nothing gentle about a north wind.

Day 192 – Always Red
Sunday, March 4, 2012, 2:15 p.m.
Sunrise: 7:15 a.m.   Sunset: 6:41 p.m.

Day 193 – Powder Kissed

Monday, March 5, 2012, 1:04 p.m.
Sunrise: 7:13 a.m.   Sunset: 6:42 p.m.

The first snow fell December 9; the last snow fell this day. The shortened season of snow lasted fewer than three months.

Day 194 – Orange Flood
Tuesday, March 6, 2012, 6:40 p.m.
Sunrise: 7:12 a.m.   Sunset: 6:43 p.m.

During a year when winter didn't deliver its usual punch, it still served up a fair share of cloudy,
cold, wet days. The beauty of this sunset said those days were over for the season.

Day 195 – Shine Through the Openings
Wednesday, March 7, 2012, 4:48 p.m.
Sunrise: 7:10 a.m.   Sunset: 6:44 p.m.

Day 196 – Sunset Spray
Thursday, March 8, 2012, 6:29 p.m.
Sunrise: 7:08 a.m.   Sunset: 6:45 p.m.

Day 197 – Pounding Surf
Friday, March 9, 2012, 1:04 p.m.
Sunrise: 7:07 a.m.   Sunset: 6:46 p.m.

A hint of ice and a splash of water; we were another day closer to spring.

Day 198 – Neighbors

Saturday, March 10, 2012, 6:42 p.m.
Sunrise: 7:05 a.m.   Sunset: 6:48 p.m.

During the warm weather months the pier is crowded with tourists. In the off-season, it's often the long-time neighbors from up the road who come to visit.

Day 199 – Bigger Than Life

Sunday, March 11, 2012, 4:24 p.m.
Sunrise: 8:03 a.m.   Sunset: 7:49 p.m.

When one looks at the lighthouses extending into the lake, it is with the realization of what a marvel it is that they were built more than 100 years ago, before the technology and equipment available today.

Day 200 – Fire Light

Monday, March 12, 2012, 7:41 p.m.
Sunrise: 8:02 a.m.   Sunset: 7:50 p.m.

Day 201 – Day of the Catch
Tuesday, March 13, 2012, 7:37 p.m.
Sunrise: 8:00 a.m.   Sunset: 7:51 p.m.

An early brush with spring encouraged some anglers off the pier and into the water in search of the perfect fishing spot.

Day 202 – 11:11
Wednesday, March 14, 2012, 11:11 a.m.
Sunrise: 7:58 a.m.   Sunset: 7:52 p.m.

Day 203 – Tranquil Intentions

Thursday, March 15, 2012, 7:57 p.m.
Sunrise: 7:57 a.m.   Sunset: 7:53 p.m.

Michigan winters can hang on well into April, so 70 degree temperatures grabbed everyone's attention.
Some lingered on the pier after sunset while a lone kayaker soaked in the evening's warmth.

Day 204 – Hugs and Kisses
Friday, March 16, 2012, 7:54 p.m.
Sunrise: 7:55 a.m.   Sunset: 7:54 p.m.

Day 205 – Just You and Me
Saturday, March 17, 2012, 7:37 p.m.
Sunrise: 7:53 a.m.   Sunset: 7:54 p.m.

A blanket to cover the still-cold sand, an evening snack, and possibly a concealed bottle of wine were the perfect accessories for date night at the beach.

Day 206 – Mirror, Mirror
Sunday, March 18, 2012, 1:16 p.m.
Sunrise: 7:51 a.m.   Sunset: 7:56 p.m.

When the lake is "like glass," conversations on the pier can be heard from the beach. This happens because the air at the surface of the water is cooler than the air above. This causes sound waves to bend down toward the water's surface by refraction for sound amplification.

Day 207 – Steel Angles
Monday, March 19, 2012, 4:54 p.m.
Sunrise: 7:50 a.m.   Sunset: 7:58 p.m.

A steel framework of isosceles triangles and trapezoids turns the
lighthouse and catwalk into a geometric study.

Day 208 – Equinox

Tuesday, March 20, 2012, 12:35 p.m.
Sunrise: 7:48 a.m.   Sunset: 7:59 p.m.

Gnarled branches and last year's beach grass seemed livelier and more hopeful
with the promise the first day of spring brought.

Day 209 – Gone Fishin'

Wednesday, March 21, 2012, 12:29 p.m.
Sunrise: 7:46 a.m.   Sunset: 8:00 p.m.

A fisherman kept the day simple with a bait bucket for a
chair, and a lighthouse as a companion.

Day 210 – Renewal

Thursday, March 22, 2012, 7:26 p.m.
Sunrise: 7:45 a.m.   Sunset: 8:01 p.m.

Day 211 – Patience

Friday, March 23, 2012, 2:50 p.m.
Sunrise: 7:43 a.m.   Sunset: 8:02 p.m.

Day 212 – Imagination's Stage

Saturday, March 24, 2012, 1:30 p.m.
Sunrise: 7:41 a.m.   Sunset: 8:03 p.m.

Cloaked in their dewy shroud, the lighthouses could ha
been the movie scene for a haunting ghost tale, murder
mystery, or a love story.

Day 213 – Swing Bridge
Sunday, March 25, 2012, 7:23 p.m.
Sunrise: 7:39 a.m.   Sunset: 8:05 p.m.

Built in 1904, the swing bridge is another structural St. Joseph icon. Every day it transports freight and passenger trains over the St. Joseph River while allowing commercial and recreational vessels access to the docks and marinas upriver.

Day 214 – End Rays

Day 215 – In the Distance
Tuesday, March 27, 2012, 8:01 p.m.
Sunrise: 7:36 a.m.   Sunset: 8:07 p.m.

Day 216 – Rose-colored Ending
Wednesday, March 28, 2012, 8:14 p.m.
Sunrise: 7:34 a.m.   Sunset: 8:08 p.m.

Day 218 – Winter Remnants
Friday, March 30, 2012, 1:33 p.m.
Sunrise: 7:31 a.m.   Sunset: 8:10 p.m.

Day 217 – Creeping
Thursday, March 29, 2012, 7:42 p.m.
Sunrise: 7:33 a.m.   Sunset: 8:09 p.m.

Day 220 – Just Breathe

Sunday, April 1, 2012, 1:31 p.m.
Sunrise: 7:27 a.m.   Sunset: 8:12 p.m.

Day 221 – Window View

Monday, April 2, 2012, 7:57 p.m.
Sunrise: 7:26 a.m.   Sunset: 8:14 p.m.

Day 219 – A-Line

Saturday, March 31, 2012, 2:44 p.m.
Sunrise: 7:29 a.m.   Sunset: 8:11 p.m.

Metal sculptures dot Silver Beach and the arboretum along the St. Joseph River as part of a public art display. The most loved metal art in town, though, continues to be the lighthouses.

Day 222 – Digging Deep, Flying High
Tuesday, April 3, 2012, 5:30 p.m.
Sunrise: 7:24 a.m.   Sunset: 8:15 p.m.

With winter a memory and the new shipping season ahead, dredging crews returned to the mouth of the St. Joseph River to finish work started in January.

Day 223 – Rich Hues
Wednesday, April 4, 2012, 8:15 p.m.
Sunrise: 7:22 a.m.   Sunset: 8:16 p.m.

Day 224 – Let the Day Begin

Thursday, April 5, 2012, 7:37 a.m.
Sunrise: 7:21 a.m.   Sunset: 8:17 p.m.

Day 225 – White Rays

Friday, April 6, 2012, 5:14 p.m.
Sunrise: 7:19 a.m.   Sunset: 8:18 p.m.

Day 226 – Rooftop Transformations

Saturday, April 7, 2012, 10:13 a.m.
The Sunrise: 7:17 a.m.   Sunset: 8:19 p.m.

In the early 20th century, the downtown bluff overlooked factories and the small homes of the people who worked there. Many structures from the past century have faded away, but the lighthouse has comfortably transitioned into a tourist landmark that completes the skyline along with the rooftop of the Silver Beach Carousel.

Day 227 – Shoot Through the Moon

Sunday, April 8, 2012, 10:04 a.m.
Sunrise: 7:16 a.m.   Sunset: 8:20 p.m.

The crescent window of *Moon Dream*, by Benik Motevosian/Genzink, frames the moods of beachfront life. The sculpture is located on Silver Beach and is part of the Krasl Art Center's permanent collection.

Day 229 – New Life

Tuesday, April 10, 2012, 10:32 a.m.
Sunrise: 7:13 a.m.   Sunset: 8:22 p.m.

Day 228 – Pier Blooms

Monday, April 9, 2012, 4:57 p.m.
Sunrise: 7:14 a.m.   Sunset: 8:21 p.m.

Surrounded by nothing but water and concrete, dandelions
demonstrated their tenacity.

Day 230 – Fire Says Goodnight

Wednesday, April 11, 2012, 8:23 p.m.
Sunrise: 7:11 a.m.   Sunset: 8:24 p.m.

Day 231 – A Job to be Done

Thursday, April 12, 2012, 8:05 p.m.
Sunrise: 7:09 a.m.   Sunset: 8:25 p.m.

Day 232 – Wire and Wood

Friday, April 13, 2012, 11:21 a.m.
Sunrise: 7:07 a.m.   Sunset: 8:26 p.m.

The beach showed signs of life as front-end loaders leveled mounds of sand that had accumulated around recently removed snow fences. The few fences that remained seemed obsolete in the springtime sun.

Day 233 – Clearing a Path
Saturday, April 14, 2012, 4:07 p.m.
Sunrise: 7:06 a.m.   Sunset: 8:27 p.m.

The U.S. Army Corps of Engineers hired MCM Marine of Sault Ste. Marie, Michigan, for a spring dredging to remove shoaling from the mouth of the St. Joseph River. The work ensured a 2012 commercial shipping season in St. Joseph's port.

Day 234 – Soar
Sunday, April 15, 2012, 4:41 p.m.
Sunrise: 7:04 a.m.   Sunset: 8:28 p.m.

The men who built the lighthouses more than a hundred years ago could have never imagined how thrill seekers would fly through the sky and skim the water tethered to a sail.

Day 235 – Tapestry of Light
Monday, April 16, 2012, 8:20 p.m.
Sunrise: 7:03 a.m.   Sunset: 8:29 p.m.

Day 236 – Surface Play
Tuesday, April 17, 2012, 8:25 p.m.
Sunrise: 7:01 a.m.   Sunset: 8:30 p.m.

Day 237 – Brushed Metal Elegance

Wednesday, April 18, 2012, 11:32 a.m.
Sunrise: 7:00 a.m.   Sunset: 8:31 p.m.

On any sunny summer day, Silver Beach would be crowded with locals and tourists. But April has a different tone. With the only sound coming from the late morning waves rolling lazily onto the sand, this moment was nestled in the protective cradle of brushed metal.

Day 238 – Maritime Billboard

Thursday, April 19, 2012, 11:54 a.m.
Sunrise: 6:58 a.m. **Sunset: 8:32 p.m.**

At some point during the previous five days, the Coast Guard added
a new message for boaters.

Day 239 – Synchronicity

Friday, April 20, 2012, 3:25 p.m.
Sunrise: 6:57 a.m. **Sunset: 8:34 p.m.**

The churning waters became a rhythmic parade of waves that marched in
precise alignment along the pier.

Day 240 – Puppy Love

Saturday, April 21, 2012, 10:48 a.m.
Sunrise: 6:55 a.m.   Sunset: 8:35 p.m.

The lighthouse is a watchful backdrop for almost every view from the downtown St. Joseph bluff.

Day 241 – Solar Flare

Sunday, April 22, 2012, 8:32 p.m.
Sunrise: 6:54 a.m.   Sunset: 8:36 p.m.

An intense north wind whipped up a spectacular wave, creating a momentary solar flare on Earth.

Day 242 – A Million Drops

Monday, April 23, 2012, 7:56 p.m.
Sunrise: 6:52 a.m.   Sunset: 8:37 p.m.

Day 243 – The Rules of Nature and Man

Tuesday, April 24, 2012, 11:53 a.m.
Sunrise: 6:51 a.m.   Sunset: 8:38 p.m.

Disobey man's rules and risk expulsion from the park. Disobey nature's rules and you may pay the ultimate price.

Day 244 – Light Side of the Storm

Wednesday, April 25, 2012, 11:41 a.m.
Sunrise: 6:49 a.m.   Sunset: 8:39 p.m.

Brightness in the eastern sky illuminated the face of the lighthouses
as stormy skies approached from the west.

Day 245 – Let's Go Bears!

Thursday, April 26, 2012, 6:15 p.m.
Sunrise: 6:48 a.m.   Sunset: 8:40 p.m.

The St. Joseph High School mascot made a split second appearance in the waves.

Day 246 – Perspectives

Friday, April 27, 2012, 2:07 p.m.
Sunrise: 6:46 a.m.   **Sunset: 8:41 p.m.**

Day 247 – Slow Awakenings

Saturday, April 28, 2012, 7:14 a.m.

Sunrise: 6:45 a.m.   Sunset: 8:42 p.m.

In the past century, hundreds of thousands of people have basked in the magic of the sun setting behind the lighthouses. Far fewer have witnessed the subtle hues and softness of sunrise as the backdrop for the lighthouses.

Day 248 – Blanket Between Heaven and Earth

Sunday, April 29, 2012, 7:46 p.m.

Sunrise: 6:44 a.m.   Sunset: 8:44 p.m.

Day 249 – Channeling
Monday, April 30, 2012, 7:58 p.m.
Sunrise: 6:42 a.m.   Sunset: 8:45 p.m.

"The first harbor to be improved along the east shore of Lake Michigan was that of Saint Joseph. The government engineers recommended that the river be straightened and this work was begun in 1836. A channel was cut across the point, the river dammed and made to wash out its own new channel to the lake." *History of St. Joseph*, L. Benj. Reber, published 1925.

Day 250 – At Rest
Tuesday, May 1, 2012, 6:34 p.m.
Sunrise: 6:41 a.m.   Sunset: 8:46 p.m.

No other humans that evening. Only ducks.

Day 251 – Dreamscape

Wednesday, May 2, 2012, 8:35 p.m.

Sunrise: 6:40 a.m.   Sunset: 8:47 p.m.

Day 252 – Definitive Strike

Thursday, May 3, 2012, 7:44 p.m.
Sunrise: 6:38 a.m.   Sunset: 8:48 p.m.

Thunder rumbles carried across the water. As the storm approached, a loud
thunder roll shook the pier. Realizing how vulnerable and exposed I was,
I redirected my momentum toward the shore. Every few yards, I turned to
survey the sky. During one of those moments, hundreds of millions of volts
of electricity connected the sky and water.

Day 254 – Together's Beginning

Saturday, May 5, 2012, 4:29 p.m.
Sunrise: 6:36 a.m.   Sunset: 8:50 p.m.

Cheers rose from the other side of the dune as a photographer captured the jubilation of a wedding party. Soon, the bridesmaids and groomsmen cleared and the photographer's attention shifted to the couple celebrating their first day as husband and wife.

Day 253 – Thick Weather

Friday, May 4, 2012, 7:31 p.m.
Sunrise: 6:37 a.m.   Sunset: 8:49 p.m.

"A lookout is maintained at all hours on the north pier. A foghorn wails its melancholy warning in times of thick weather," *History of St. Joseph*, L. Benj. Reber, published 1925.

Day 255 – Resilience

Sunday, May 6, 2012, 4:34 p.m.
Sunrise: 6:34 a.m.   Sunset: 8:51 p.m.

A single blade of beach grass that survived autumn winds, winter ice, and spring rains delivered inspiration.

Day 256 – Invitation of a Gray Day

Monday, May 7, 2012, 5:31 p.m.
Sunrise: 6:33 a.m.   Sunset: 8:52 p.m.

The rain washed distractions away and whispers of "come closer" beckoned.

Day 257 – Spring Green

Tuesday, May 8, 2012, 8:06 p.m.
Sunrise: 6:32 a.m.   Sunset: 8:53 p.m.

Day 258 – Immeasurably Extended in Time
Wednesday, May 9, 2012, 5:44 p.m.
Sunrise: 6:31 a.m.   Sunset: 8:54 p.m.

The magic of a photograph is its ability to suspend a moment
for the rest of time.

Day 259 – Tell Me a Story
Thursday, May 10, 2012, 8:44 p.m.
Sunrise: 6:30 a.m.   Sunset: 8:56 p.m.

Every well-earned rusted blemish tells the story of countless
storms, cocoons of ice, and days of blazing sun.

Day 260 – Shimmering Prize

Friday, May 11, 2012, 8:07 p.m.
Sunrise: 6:29 a.m.   Sunset: 8:57 p.m.

The inner lighthouse's Fresnel lens is believed to have been made between 1884 and 1886, and likely installed in 1907; it survived a century of the elements before being rescued for restoration.

Day 261 – Through the Keyhole

Saturday, May 12, 2012, 6:03 p.m.
Sunrise: 6:28 a.m.   Sunset: 8:58 p.m.

Day 262 – On the Run

Sunday, May 13, 2012, 2:45 p.m.
Sunrise: 6:27 a.m.   Sunset: 8:59 p.m.

As people fished and took a Mother's Day stroll on the pier, a very young and scared woodchuck found himself in the middle of it all. He ran from one side of the pier bound by the river, to the other side bound by a beach filled with people enjoying the weather. After several trips back and forth, he settled on cowering under the blue railing until he could safely escape.

Day 263 – Shades of Marmalade
Monday, May 14, 2012, 8:58 p.m.
Sunrise: 6:25 a.m.   Sunset: 9:00 p.m.

Day 264 – Angry Bird

Tuesday, May 15, 2012, 6:58 a.m.
Sunrise: 6:24 a.m.   Sunset: 9:01 p.m.

Seagulls start their day with the sun. This guy got up on the wrong side of the rail.

Day 265 – Backlit Splendor
Wednesday, May 16, 2012, 8:39 p.m.
Sunrise: 6:24 a.m.   **Sunset: 9:02 p.m.**

Day 266 – Peace
Thursday, May 17, 2012, 8:49 p.m.
Sunrise: 6:23 a.m.   **Sunset: 9:03 p.m.**

"When the river had been straightened, a timber revetment was made across the sand pit and two piers constructed. The north pier was eleven hundred feet long; the south pier two hundred feet long,"
History of St. Joseph, L. Benj. Reber, published 1925.

Day 268 – First Date

Saturday, May 19, 2012, 8:49 p.m.
Sunrise: 6:21 a.m.   Sunset: 9:05 p.m.

Imagine how many couples have talked through the excited energy of a first date while walking in the shadow of the lighthouses.

Day 267 – Morning Meditation

Friday, May 18, 2012, 6:53 a.m.
Sunrise: 6:22 a.m.   Sunset: 9:04 p.m.

Day 269 – Beach Ballet

Sunday, May 20, 2012, 9:32 a.m.
Sunrise: 6:20 a.m.   Sunset: 9:06 p.m.

Day 270 – The Promise of Tomorrow
Monday, May 21, 2012, 8:58 p.m.
Sunrise: 6:19 a.m.   Sunset: 9:07 p.m.

Sunset isn't the end. Its radiance is a sneak peek at the gift the next day brings.

Day 271 – Lift Off
Tuesday, May 22, 2012, 7:59 p.m.
Sunrise: 6:18 a.m.   Sunset: 9:08 p.m.

Day 272 – Blissful Blue Illusion
Wednesday, May 23, 2012, 11:44 a.m.
Sunrise: 6:18 a.m.   Sunset: 9:08 p.m.

Day 273 – Blue and Silver Currents
Thursday, May 24, 2012, 4:34 p.m.
Sunrise: 6:17 a.m.   Sunset: 9:09 p.m.

The sunlight exposed the chameleon quality of the water once again: silver on one side, blue on the other.

Day 274 – Fresh Air
Friday, May 25, 2012, 7:39 a.m.
Sunrise: 6:16 a.m.   Sunset: 9:10 p.m.

Day 275 – Eager Anticipation
Saturday, May 26, 2012, 3:49 p.m.
Sunrise: 6:15 a.m.   Sunset: 9:11 p.m.

After months of cold winds, an overcast day didn't deter those hungry for summer.

Day 276 – Warm View

Sunday, May 27, 2012, 9:10 p.m.
Sunrise: 6:15 a.m.　　　Sunset: 9:12 p.m.

Day 277 – Cool View

Monday, May 28, 2012, 8:43 p.m.
Sunrise: 6:14 a.m.　　　Sunset: 9:13 p.m.

Day 278 – Only the Moment Matters
Tuesday, May 29, 2012, 6:58 a.m.
Sunrise: 6:14 a.m.   Sunset: 9:14 p.m.

Day 279 – Wednesday Night Sailing Club
Wednesday, May 30, 2012, 8:09 p.m.
Sunrise: 6:13 a.m.   Sunset: 9:14 p.m.

Local sailors don't wait for the weekend to reach for freedom on Lake Michigan. From late spring through early fall, they test their nautical skill in a friendly, after-work sailing race each Wednesday night. Weather permitting, of course.

Day 280 – Tracks in the Sand
Thursday, May 31, 2012, 7:21 p.m.
Sunrise: 6:13 a.m.   Sunset: 9:15 p.m.

Day 282 – Geronimo
Saturday, June 2, 2012, 12:18 p.m.
Sunrise: 6:12 a.m.   Sunset: 9:17 p.m.

Squall gear, a healthy grip on the rail, and the heart of a warrior were all that was needed to take on the choppy waters of a chilly June weekend.

Day 281 – Restless
Friday, June 1, 2012, 4:56 p.m.
Sunrise: 6:12 a.m.   Sunset: 9:16 p.m.

There are no hard lines between the seasons. It's a push and pull of cold and warmth, sun and clouds, even when the calendar says summer is near.

Day 283 – Spotlight
Sunday, June 3, 2012, 9:03 p.m.
Sunrise: 6:11 a.m.   Sunset: 9:17 p.m.

Day 284 – Late in the Sunlight

Monday, June 4, 2012, 9:13 p.m.
Sunrise: 6:11 a.m.   Sunset: 9:18 p.m.

Twilight: the last breath of day and the first life of night.

Day 285 – Closed In
Tuesday, June 5, 2012, 9:20 p.m.
Sunrise: 6:11 a.m.   Sunset: 9:19 p.m.

Day 286 – A Helping Hand
Wednesday, June 6, 2012, 9:17 p.m.
Sunrise: 6:10 a.m.   Sunset: 9:19 p.m.

The Wednesday night sailing race closed with a failed engine and a friendly tow back to the marina.

Day 287 – Laughs and Love

Thursday, June 7, 2012, 9:18 p.m.
Sunrise: 6:10 a.m.   Sunset: 9:20 p.m.

Dozens of people. Dozens of viewpoints. Just one sunset.

Day 288 – Uncomplicated Friday

Friday, June 8, 2012, 2:44 p.m.
Sunrise: 6:10 a.m.   Sunset: 9:21 p.m.

Day 289 – Beachgoers Delight

Saturday, June 9, 2012, 11:39 a.m.
Sunrise: 6:10 a.m.   Sunset: 9:21 p.m.

Day 290 – Shadows of Former Days

Sunday, June 10, 2012, 9:56 a.m.
Sunrise: 6:09 a.m.   Sunset: 9:22 p.m.

The lighthouses once stood in the shadow of a visitors' playground – Silver Beach Amusement Park. Year by year, piece by piece, the park disappeared, including the Shadowland Ballroom. Interest in the beachfront as a gathering place returned and The Shadowland Pavilion was built, in homage to the original ballroom, bringing music and performance back to the lake shore.

Day 291 – On Duty

Monday, June 11, 2012, 1:04 p.m.
Sunrise: 6:09 a.m.   Sunset: 9:22 p.m.

The green flag signaled that it was safe to go into the water, but cool temperatures
kept beach goers away from Silver Beach.

Day 292 – Wave Jumper

Tuesday, June 12, 2012, 3:17 p.m.
Sunrise: 6:09 a.m.   Sunset: 9:23 p.m.

Freedom: best enjoyed from the top of the wave.

Day 293 – Big Life

Wednesday, June 13, 2012, 8:17 p.m.
Sunrise: 6:09 a.m.   Sunset: 9:23 p.m.

Harnessing the wind makes life bigger.

Day 294 – Dune View
Thursday, June 14, 2012, 9:22 p.m.
Sunrise: 6:09 a.m.   **Sunset: 9:24 p.m.**

"In 1863, a new survey was made by Colonel Reynolds. The river is reported in that survey as being 212 feet wide, with a channel depth of 12 feet. The south pier was extended two hundred feet at this time. Up to 1879, the government had spent over a hundred thousand dollars on this harbor." *History of St. Joseph*, L. Benj. Reber, published 1925.

Day 295 – Linger
Friday, June 15, 2012, 9:03 p.m.
Sunrise: 6:09 a.m.   **Sunset: 9:24 p.m.**

Day 297 – Rocket Ship

Sunday, June 17, 2012, 11:19 a.m.
Sunrise: 6:09 a.m.   Sunset: 9:25 p.m.

A boy and his mom walked toward the beach with their chairs and a cooler in tow. As they came over the dune and saw the lake stretched out ahead of them, the boy excitedly exclaimed, "There it is! There's the rocket ship!" Hearing his view of the lighthouse made me see it differently.

Day 296 – Pinwheel

Saturday, June 16, 2012, 12:20 p.m.
Sunrise: 6:09 a.m.   Sunset: 9:24 p.m.

Day 298 – Moment of Discovery

Monday, June 18, 2012, 8:44 p.m.
Sunrise: 6:09 a.m.   Sunset: 9:25 p.m.

Day 299 – The Hangout
Tuesday, June 19, 2012, 9:13 p.m.
Sunrise: 6:10 a.m.   Sunset: 9:25 p.m.

Face-to-face laughter, not "LOL." In person introductions instead of "friend requests." Real fun, no virtual games. Lake Michigan: the original social network.

Day 300 – Summer: First Morning

Wednesday, June 20, 2012, 8:06 a.m.
Sunrise: 6:10 a.m.   Sunset: 9:26 p.m.

On the shortest, darkest day, it is the promise of this first summer morning
each year that gives hope.

Day 301 – Stretching to Forever

Thursday, June 21, 2012, 9:23 p.m.
Sunrise: 6:10 a.m.   Sunset: 9:26 p.m.

With an outstretched arm to the western sky, the shore sent the last rays of light beyond the horizon.

Day 302 – Eclectic Rays

Friday, June 22, 2012, 9:02 p.m.
Sunrise: 6:10 a.m.   Sunset: 9:26 p.m.

Day 303 – Escape

Saturday, June 23, 2012, 10:48 a.m.
Sunrise: 6:11 a.m.   Sunset: 9:26 p.m.

Day 304 – Red Suits It
Sunday, June 24, 2012, 8:38 a.m.
Sunrise: 6:11 a.m.   Sunset: 9:26 p.m.

Day 305 – Out of Season
Monday, June 25, 2012, 8:27 p.m.
Sunrise: 6:11 a.m.   Sunset: 9:26 p.m.

It was strange weather for June. The northwest wind and the
bite in the wind felt like the approach of autumn instead of
the first days of summer.

Day 306 – Watching the Show
Tuesday, June 26, 2012, 9:19 p.m.
Sunrise: 6:12 a.m.   Sunset: 9:26 p.m.

Sunset unfolds differently each night; unscripted and spontaneous,
yet comfortingly familiar.

Day 307 – Lead the Way
Wednesday, June 27, 2012, 8:06 p.m.
Sunrise: 6:12 a.m.   Sunset: 9:26 p.m.

For centuries, the wind has pushed man in his effort to transport,
discover, and reach intended destinations. Equally powerful is its ability
to pull people together in a common love of the water.

Day 308 – Awaken from These Dreams

Thursday, June 28, 2012, 6:29 a.m.
Sunrise: 6:12 a.m.   Sunset: 9:26 p.m.

e sunrise was magical. The cool air still held nighttime's clammy
dampness. All was quiet except for an ambitious fisherman
and seagulls searching for breakfast.

Day 309 – Prepare for Battle

Friday, June 29, 2012, 10:33 a.m.
Sunrise: 6:13 a.m.   Sunset: 9:26 p.m.

Workers built sand berms to transform the beach into a World War II battle zone where Pacific and European beach invasions would be re-enacted. The next day Lest We Forget, a southwest Michigan organization dedicated to honoring U.S. military veterans, staged the ambitious event to keep alive the memory of the sacrifices so many have made for our freedom.

Day 310 – Beach Invasion

Saturday, June 30, 2012, 12:01 p.m.
Sunrise: 6:13 a.m.   Sunset: 9:26 p.m.

Allied forces landed on Tiscornia Beach to re-create the Pacific theater battle at Iwo Jima. Vintage aircraft flew overhead as pyrotechnics simulated the bombing for thousands of spectators who looked on from the pier.

Day 311 – Blaze
Sunday, July 1, 2012, 9:06 p.m.
Sunrise: 6:14 a.m. **Sunset: 9:26 p.m.**

Day 312 – Heading Home
Monday, July 2, 2012, 8:42 p.m.
Sunrise: 6:14 a.m. Sunset: 9:26 p.m.

Day 313 – Celebration Preparations
Tuesday, July 3, 2012, 10:17 a.m.
Sunrise: 6:15 a.m.   Sunset: 9:25 p.m.

Independence Day is celebrated each year with a spectacular firework display launched from the pier.
To keep the festivities safe, everyone must stay back.

Day 314 – Inner Light

Wednesday, July 4, 2012, 10:23 a.m.
Sunrise: 6:16 a.m.   Sunset: 9:25 p.m.

Without a single word, the lighthouse tells its story of a thousand thunderstorms, a million minutes in the snowfall, and year upon year of crashing waves.

Day 315 – Outer Light
Thursday, July 5, 2012, 8:51 a.m.
Sunrise: 6:16 a.m.   Sunset: 9:25 p.m.

Although it is the smallest of the pair, the outer beacon endures
the most punishment. Its position at the end of the pier exposes it
to undiluted waves from the south, west, and north that can crash
a dozen or more feet above its spire.

TO ENERGIZE THE FOG
SIGNAL KEY YOUR
MICROPHONE FIVE
TIMES ON CHANNEL 83A

Day 316 – Sizzle

Friday, July 6, 2012, 9:09 p.m.
Sunrise: 6:17 a.m.   Sunset: 9:24 p.m.

Day 317 – Forever Starts Here

Saturday, July 7, 2012, 8:07 a.m.
Sunrise: 6:17 a.m.   Sunset: 9:24 p.m.

Guests gathered in the parking lot. Family members huddled together for photos on the pier. The beach would soon play host to a wedding with the lighthouses standing in witness.

Day 318 – Summer Breezes

Sunday, July 8, 2012, 9:08 p.m.
Sunrise: 6:18 a.m.   Sunset: 9:24 p.m.

Day 319 – Textures

Monday, July 9, 2012, 9:21 p.m.
Sunrise: 6:19 a.m.   Sunset: 9:23 p.m.

"The harbor at this writing is one of the best on the lakes, with constant improvement carried on as a matter of course. The piers are being rebuilt of reinforced concrete as the original timbers were beginning to crumble with age and the constant pounding of the waves." *History of St. Joseph*, L. Benj. Reber, published 1925.

Day 320 – Friends

Tuesday, July 10, 2012, 9:02 p.m.
Sunrise: 6:20 a.m.   Sunset: 9:23 p.m.

Growing up here is special. Memories created here with our friends last a lifetime.

Day 321 – Wind Spirit
Wednesday, July 11, 2012, 8:17 p.m.
Sunrise: 6:20 a.m.   Sunset: 9:22 p.m.

Standing on the south pier, we watched the sailboats cross the finish line of their weekly race.
One boat approached the pier at a high rate of speed. We all jumped back but the man at the
helm kept the boat in full control as he sped past a few feet from the edge of the pier.

Day 322 – Clean Sweep
Thursday, July 12, 2012, 8:06 p.m.
Sunrise: 6:21 a.m.   Sunset: 9:22 p.m.

Before the beach bums, tourists, and sun seekers arrived, city workers swept the sand
clean of the remnants from the prior day.

Day 323 – Dog Days
Friday, July 13, 2012, 5:40 p.m.
Sunrise: 6:22 a.m.   Sunset: 9:21 p.m.

Sluggish, muggy heat brought people in search of the cooling relief of the
water, but the heavy air followed and slowed the speed of life.

Day 324 – Unity
Saturday, July 14, 2012, 5:35 p.m.
Sunrise: 6:23 a.m.   Sunset: 9:21 p.m.

One day
One moment
One love

Day 325 – Childhood Summer

Sunday, July 15, 2012, 9:17 p.m.
Sunrise: 6:23 a.m.   Sunset: 9:20 p.m.

Their mom sat on the beach taking photos, while the trio of kids hammed it up.
Their infectious laughter was the sound of summer.

Day 326 – Cooler by the Lake
Monday, July 16, 2012, 7:46 a.m.
Sunrise: 6:24 a.m.   Sunset: 9:19 p.m.

Day 327 – It Hangs in the Air
Tuesday, July 17, 2012, 8:52 p.m.
Sunrise: 6:25 a.m.   Sunset: 9:19 p.m.

Sunset secrets were soon hushed by guardian cloud cover.

Day 328 – Ladder to the Sun
Wednesday, July 18, 2012, 8:01 p.m.
Sunrise: 6:26 a.m.   Sunset: 9:18 p.m.

From here, it was only a short climb to the sun king.

Day 330 – King's Gold

Friday, July 20, 2012, 9:09 p.m.
Sunrise: 6:28 a.m.   Sunset: 9:16 p.m.

Day 329 – Summer Nights

Thursday, July 19, 2012, 7:56 p.m.
Sunrise: 6:27 a.m.   Sunset: 9:17 p.m.

Heavy clouds suggested spring or fall. The muggy scent, the echoes of gulls,
and the sticky heat told the real story.

Day 331 – Pastel Palette
Saturday, July 21, 2012, 9:16 p.m.
Sunrise: 6:29 a.m.   Sunset: 9:15 p.m.

Day 332 – It's a Beautiful Morning
Sunday, July 22, 2012, 9:55 a.m.
Sunrise: 6:30 a.m.   Sunset: 9:15 p.m.

Day 333 – Rainbow Ending

Monday, July 23, 2012, 9:00 p.m.
Sunrise: 6:31 a.m.   Sunset: 9:14 p.m.

Day 334 – Layered

Tuesday, July 24, 2012, 8:52 p.m.
Sunrise: 6:31 a.m.   Sunset: 9:13 p.m.

The intricate cloud formation unfolded quickly. It recreated itself with unusual speed, catching the attention of everyone including seasoned dune sitters and pier walkers.

Day 335 – Pointing to the Top

Wednesday, July 25, 2012, 8:14 a.m.
Sunrise: 6:32 a.m.   Sunset: 9:12 p.m.

"The steel superstructure of the new tower is held by 12,000 rivets. The concrete foundation is of double walls and supported by steel pilings." Tuesday, September 10, 1907 – *News-Palladium*

Day 336 – Pure Energy

Thursday, July 26, 2012, 7:43 p.m.
Sunrise: 6:33 a.m.   Sunset: 9:11 p.m.

The midnight blue storm clouds blowing in from the west were too good to pass up. A sprint up the back of the dune revealed a tempest in the making.

Day 337 – Plunge
Friday, July 27, 2012, 9:03 p.m.
Sunrise: 6:34 a.m.   Sunset: 9:10 p.m.

The fishermen quipped one to the other. "If they drown, it's their own fault." "I told them they have no business out there." They were talking about the three teen boys jumping off the pier. When the boys hit the water, the waves fueled by the north wind shoved them back to the side of the pier. They crawled up the ladder, resting with hands on knees. Catching their breath for just a minute each time, they jumped over and over. There were no headlines the next morning; they must have made it home safely.

Day 338 – Deep Blue Vista

Saturday, July 28, 2012, 7:53 a.m.
Sunrise: 6:35 a.m.   Sunset: 9:09 p.m.

Day 339 – On Edge

Sunday, July 29, 2012, 8:01 p.m.
Sunrise: 6:36 a.m.   Sunset: 9:08 p.m.

As you look at the curve of the sheet metal and the rivets that hold it all together, think for a moment about the men who built these structures. Could they have imagined that what they were building would be standing strong a century later? Would they have been surprised that something with such utilitarian beginnings would be loved by so many.

Day 340 – On the Shelf

Monday, July 30, 2012, 8:58 p.m.

Sunrise: 6:37 a.m. **Sunset: 9:07 p.m.**

Patience: having the faith to let the perfect moment come to you.

Day 341 – Lake Michigan Bike Trail

Tuesday, July 31, 2012, 8:46 p.m.
Sunrise: 6:38 a.m.   Sunset: 9:06 p.m.

The low roar of the waves mixed with the loud, excited chatter of the two teenage girls. They paused for a moment before walking their bikes beyond railing at the mid-point of the pier. Their sense of adventure was tempered by respect for the waves. They went no further than this.

Day 342 – Wednesday at the Races
Wednesday, August 1, 2012, 8:05 p.m.
Sunrise: 6:39 a.m.   Sunset: 9:04 p.m.

Calm waters don't rock the boat, but they don't speed it along either.

Day 343 – Gone to Seed
Thursday, August 2, 2012, 8:49 p.m.
Sunrise: 6:40 a.m.   Sunset: 9:03 p.m.

Spring is the promise of the potential of new life.
Late summer is promises fulfilled.

Day 344 – Standout

Friday, August 3, 2012, 1:08 p.m.
Sunrise: 6:41 a.m.   Sunset: 9:02 p.m.

Only seeking the easy angles leaves perspectives unexplored. See things with new eyes.

Day 345 – Threatening Energy

Saturday, August 4, 2012, 6:41 p.m.
Sunrise: 6:42 a.m.   Sunset: 9:01 p.m.

The idea of standing on the beach to watch a storm role in was empowering, until it was time to do it. Growling thunder, fast moving clouds, and off-shore lighting created an awe inspiring but intimidating atmosphere.

Day 346 – Fantail Shrimp

Sunday, August 5, 2012, 10:59 a.m.
Sunrise: 6:43 a.m.   Sunset: 9:00 p.m.

A night of storms brought a morning of west winds and clear air.

Day 347 – In the Evening
Monday, August 6, 2012, 8:41 p.m.
Sunrise: 6:44 a.m.   Sunset: 8:58 p.m.

"Teetering on its foundations, weakened at every new onslaught of the waves, and the fear of the keepers during every storm, the decrepit wooden lighthouse at the end of the north pier is to go. In its place is being reared a steel tower 52 feet in height, seated on a concrete base and strong enough to defy the sea for a century to come." Tuesday, September 10, 1907 – *News-Palladium*

Day 348 – Center Star

Tuesday, August 7, 2012, 8:48 p.m.

Sunrise: 6:45 a.m.   Sunset: 8:57 p.m.

Flowing robes in tow, Earth's power star awed its audience during sky flight.

Day 349 – Get to Work

Wednesday, August 8, 2012, 7:48 a.m.
Sunrise: 6:46 a.m.   Sunset: 8:56 p.m.

Day 350 – Fade to Gray

Thursday, August 9, 2012, 7:53 p.m.
Sunrise: 6:48 a.m.   Sunset: 8:54 p.m.

Many think this is a black and white photo. If you look closely, you'll see the red roof of the lighthouse. It was simply an exceptionally gray day.

Day 351 – In Search of Surf

Friday, August 10, 2012, 5:43 p.m.
Sunrise: 6:49 a.m.   Sunset: 8:52 p.m.

As sand and water spray swirled in the air, two young men ran the length of the pier, clutching surfboards. One led the other in the sprint to harness the energy.

Day 352 – Rest in Peace

Saturday, August 11, 2012, 1:21 p.m.
Sunrise: 6:50 a.m.   Sunset: 8:52 p.m.

After an afternoon of shooting rough waters, a photo review session revealed an unexpected story.
Unnoticed as the shot was taken, a family, maybe friends, released their loved one into the arms of Lake Michigan.

Day 353 – Solitude
Sunday, August 12, 2012, 7:52 p.m.
Sunrise: 6:51 a.m.   Sunset: 8:50 p.m.

"The replacing of the wooden lighthouse with a steel tower is in line with the general policy of the lighthouse service on the lakes. Similar structures have been completed at Michigan City, Holland, and other ports on Lake Michigan." Tuesday, September 10, 1907 – *News-Palladium*

Day 354 – Union of Sky and Water
Monday, August 13, 2012, 8:25 p.m.
Sunrise: 6:52 a.m.   Sunset: 8:49 p.m.

Day 355 – Sunset Keeper
Tuesday, August 14, 2012, 8:24 p.m.
Sunrise: 6:53 a.m.   Sunset: 8:47 p.m.

When this photo was taken, the lighthouses were still in the possession of the United States Government. In 2013, it granted ownership of the lighthouses to the City of St. Joseph.

Day 356 – Quietly, It Calls
Wednesday, August 15, 2012, 8:38 p.m.
Sunrise: 6:54 a.m.   Sunset: 8:46 p.m.

Day 357 – The Timing of a Sign
Thursday, August 16, 2012, 7:29 a.m.
Sunrise: 6:55 a.m.   Sunset: 8:44 p.m.

The first eleven months of this project included several unsuccessful attempts to frame the St. Joseph Harbor Navigation Project sign with the lighthouse. Then, someone moved it with just days left in the project.

Day 358 – Dream Pillows
Friday, August 17, 2012, 7:35 a.m.
Sunrise: 6:56 a.m.   Sunset: 8:43 p.m.

The views from Tiscornia Park are some of the most scenic of the lighthouse. The park was donated to the City of St. Joseph on March 16, 1964, by Lester Tiscornia and Auto Specialties. The company had leased it to the City for a decade for the sum of $1 per year until the time of the donation.

Day 359 – Strength and Endurance

Saturday, August 18, 2012, 10:58 a.m.

Sunrise: 6:57 a.m.   Sunset: 8:41 p.m.

More than 1,500 athletes from across the country flocked to southwest Michigan for the Ironman Steelhead 70.3 Triathlon. They came to vie for one of the coveted Ironman 70.3 World Championship qualifying spots.

Day 360 – Warrior March
Sunday, August 19, 2012, 8:00 a.m.
Sunrise: 6:58 a.m.   Sunset: 8:40 p.m.

The 1.2 mile swim in the clear Lake Michigan waters off of Tiscornia and Jean Klock parks kicked off the Steelhead Triathlon.
Athletes were divided by gender and age into groups distinguished by brightly colored swim caps.

Day 361 – The Artist's Signature

Monday, August 20, 2012, 8:32 p.m.
Sunrise: 6:59 a.m.   Sunset: 8:38 p.m.

A brush stroke here, a splash of color there and a new masterpiece was created, never to be duplicated.

Day 362 – Sunset Daze

Tuesday, August 21, 2012, 8:37 p.m.
Sunrise: 7:00 a.m.   Sunset: 8:37 p.m.

"With the establishment of the new tower, a new beacon light will be
placed in position and lamps of greater magnitude provided for the
towers. The beacon, or range light, is to be a 21-foot tower at the end of
the pier. It will be provided with a red light of the sixth order."
Tuesday, September 10, 1907 – *News-Palladium*

Day 364 – The Sporting Life
Thursday, August 23, 2012, 8:12 p.m.
Sunrise: 7:02 a.m.   Sunset: 8:34 p.m.

Day 363 – Returning to Port
Wednesday, August 22, 2012, 7:34 p.m.
Sunrise: 7:01 a.m.   Sunset: 8:35 p.m.

Day 365 – Safe Passage

Friday, August 24, 2012, 7:50 a.m.
Sunrise: 7:03 a.m.   Sunset: 8:32 p.m.

The stairs to the catwalk were removed long ago. The boards that created the walkway between the steel beams are gone too.
Yet the catwalk completes the lighthouses and adds to their uniqueness.

Day 366 – Grand Style
Saturday, August 25, 2012, 11:08 a.m.
Sunrise: 7:04 a.m.   Sunset: 8:31 p.m.

The Sam Laud eased into port and engrossed an audience on both piers with its steady
maneuvering of the channel. The 634-foot freighter was first launched in 1975 and can
carry up to 23,700 tons of cargo.

View366

A Year-long Visual Story of the St. Joseph Lighthouses

Bonus Photos

The collection of photos from the year of shooting goes well beyond what could be held in a single book. Sometimes selecting "the" photo for the day was easy. Some days, it was nearly impossible to choose. Other days held special moments that were not in the same sightline as the lighthouses but were part of the experience. A few of these photos are featured in the front of the book as well as in this bonus section.

Day 329 – A Cool Drink on a Summer Morning

Thursday, July 19, 2012, 8:02 a.m.
Sunrise: 6:27 a.m.   Sunset: 9:17 p.m.

I visited the pier twice this day. The morning shots of the lighthouse didn't interest me much and I knew I'd be back in the evening. As I turned to return to my car, I noticed two visitors out for a refreshing morning drink.

Day 139 – Snowy Owl

Wednesday, January 11, 2012, 5:23 p.m.
Sunrise: 8:13 a.m.   Sunset: 5:35 p.m.

A stunning sunset and a watchful visit from a snowy owl perched in a tree next to the pier made this one of the most memorable days of photography for me during the entire project.

Day 351 – A Moment of Awe

Friday, August 10, 2012, 5:43 p.m.
Sunrise: 6:49 a.m.   Sunset: 8:52 p.m.

After running the length of the pier, the surfer marveled for a moment
at the waves he was about to ride.

Day 359 – Old Glory
Saturday, August 18, 2012, 11:02 a.m.
Sunrise: 6:57 a.m.   Sunset: 8:41 p.m.

Day 360 – Photo Bomb
Sunday, August 19, 2012, 7:58 a.m.
Sunrise: 6:58 a.m.   Sunset: 8:40 p.m.

As I photographed the lighthouse through the next group of Ironman Steelhead Triathlon competitors waiting to jump into the water, two of them decided there was plenty of time for a quick photo bomb.